CONTENTS

CONTENT WARNING:
Please be aware that this volume of Heartstopper
contains discussion of an eating disorder and one mention
of self-harm. For a more detailed description of this content,
please visit: aliceoseman.com/content-warnings

✳ Not caught up with the story so far?
Read chapters 1 & 2 in VOLUME 1
and chapter 3 in VOLUME 2!

Sunday 23rd May

So... I came out as bisexual to my mum.

It feels like it's all happened so fast... but so much has happened. It's less than two months since me and Charlie kissed for the first (and second) time,

then started sort of going out (aka

LOTS. MORE. KISSING.)

You're amazing

and then I spent some time trying to figure out my sexuality... which still feels kinda confusing sometimes!! Sexuality is COMPLICATED. But 'bisexual' feels right. ☺

I looked up what bisexual means

And now we're officially <u>boyfriends</u>. That feels so awesome to say.

I HAVE A BOYFRIEND!!!!
(and he's amazing ♥)

And now we're gonna tell people

We said we might start telling our friends and people at school, but... how would we do that?? No one even knows I like guys. And Charlie got bullied pretty badly when he was outed last year.

Maybe it'd be better to keep it a secret for a bit longer...

4.OUT

566

Oh my god

How'd it go?

Yeah??

Really good! She was really supportive!

Yeah!

Want a well done kiss? ♥

Yeah...

Oh, Nick's definitely banned from sleepovers forever now.

WHAT!!

Yup. There will be _no_ hanky panky in this house.

Please don't say "hanky panky".

SIP

Bedroom door open at all times!!

I've got to go, I have an exam

No hanky panky until you're married!!

Stop saying "hanky panky"

They were fine about it but I think you're banned from sleepovers

What!?

It's not like we'd... do anything!

Anyway... you've got your English exam today?

Yeah...

I'll... meet you after?

Yeah!!

574

JUNE

Thursday 3 June
11:16

Charlie 🐻
How was your chemistry exam??

Not too bad, but... not great 😅
Are you on study leave? Can
you come round mine? I badly
need hugs

580

586

Huh? Why?

Well... I've sort of been stressed out because of exams and...

being fully out as a couple... everyone talking about us... I think that would finish me off

ha ha

You can talk to me about it...?

Can you just... kiss me more...

590

591

594

I'd, uh... I'd also recommend finding somewhere a little more discreet to make out with your boyfriend.

I'm glad Charlie's settled into the team. I've been keeping an eye on him. I know he's been a target of some pretty severe bullying in the past.

If I hear you've done anything to hurt him, we'll be having words, all right?

Y-yeah- I mean- I wouldn't-

598

599

What was that all about?

THE NEXT MORNING...

SIT

...Nick? Are you okay?

Late night

How come??

Meh, my brother's home and he's being <u>shitty</u>.

I don't... really... wanna talk about it...

Well... I had something I wanted to ask you...

607

609

614

615

Good evening, Year 10s and 11s of Truham and Higgs, and good evening parents!

We've got a lot of information to get through this evening.

My name is Mr Ajayi! I teach art at Higgs.

And I'm Mr Farouk. I teach physics at Truham.

We'll tell them after the talk

Yeah...

We'll be supervising the Paris trip this year...

Now, we need one person from each group to come up to the front to write down your names.

Us four, then?

Oh - are you going up to the front?

Yeah!

"You haven't been quite as subtle as you think you have."

"Elle knows too. I think we worked it out when we all went bowling."

"But—"

"Don't tell Tao yet."

What? Why??

He...he might have been the reason you got outed last year.

It was an accident! We were just chatting in the corridor... he was saying how happy he was that you decided to tell us...

...but someone might have overheard.

He would never ever tell anyone deliberately, but he's loud and chatty and can't keep secrets.

Don't tell him right before the Paris trip.

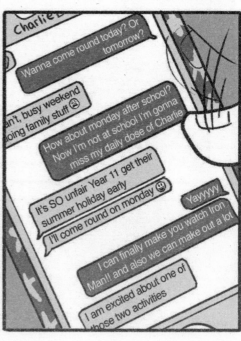

629

Exactly.

At the time, there weren't any other out gay kids in school, so it was the most exciting news of the week.

People either thought I was a novelty or I was just gross. It... it really suprised me how many people are still homophobic.

They'd tell me I was disgusting. Right to my face.

640

645

650

WHUMP

!!

 SHIT sorry I meant to message you!!!

My brother's being a dick, he literally won't stop pestering me

Might be better if you don't come round here until he's back at uni

 It was my fault for not telling him sooner tbh

No! You shouldn't have to tell him if you didn't want to

 I guess he would have found out eventually one way or another. I should probably call my dad soon and tell him too

You don't have to! you can take your time!

 I want him to know about you!! Plus I want to be the one to tell him, not David

I'm so sorry, this is all my fault

You shouldn't have to feel rushed or pressured by anybody

Charlie this is NOT your fault!!!!!!!!

Coming out is HARD and COMPLICATED, right???

And it doesn't all happen at once! And it doesn't always go right! Sometimes it probably doesn't even happen at all!! Coming out to my mum was amazing but I never expected it to go super well with everyone!! And it's not YOUR fault!
I just want people to know who I am and know that you're my boyfriend and I know that not everyone will like it but I'm ready for that. We're probably gonna have to come out hundreds more times in our lives!!

It might be shitty sometimes but I promise I'm okay

And it's all worth it

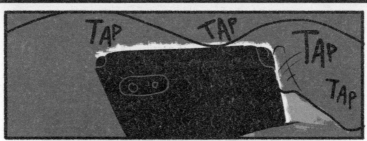

658

659

ONE WEEK LATER

664

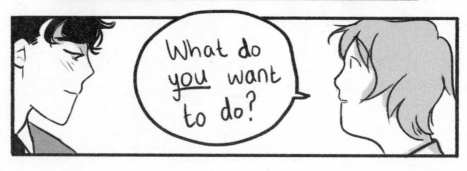

I just...

I don't want what happened to me to happen to Nick

...

Anyway... tell me about this boy

Wha- no

Come onnn... not even his name?

Um... it's Daniel...

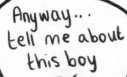

I didn't know Harry was coming on this trip...

Yeah... It'll be fine. He's been ignoring us since what happened at the cinema.

671

613

You're in room 414. I'll be in 403 if you need me. But hopefully you won't.

And meet back here at 7 for dinner.

Mr Ajayi, where are you sleeping?

I'll be sharing with Youssef- uh, I mean, Mr Farouk

keys

réception

Which floor?

4!

It's here!

414

Oh... we have to share beds?

Yeah...

Well, I want the window bed.

Well I want the other bed, then! I hate getting woken up by the sun.

Um... I guess ...I'll go with Tao and you go with Aled?

Yeah...

679

KNOCK KNOCK KNOCK

Aled? Is this your room? I still have your phone charger!

Oh!! Just coming!

WOAH your room is so small

Thanks for letting me use it!

No prob!

Is Elle out there?? Tell me if Elle is out there!!

I can't wait to do it with you one day

Y-Yeah

CLICK

684

685

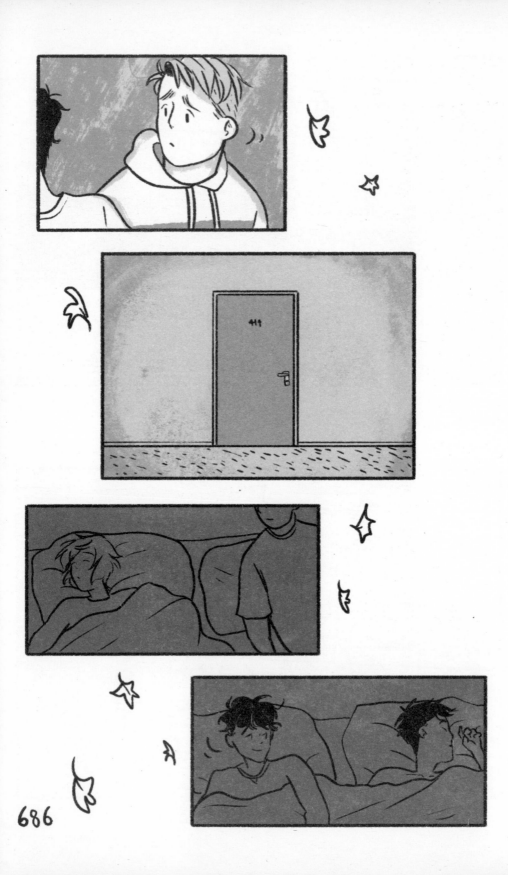

694

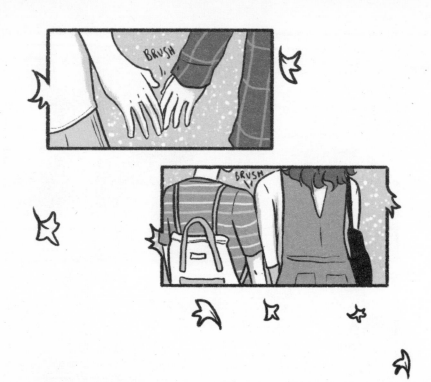

Char? Do you want an ice cream?

Oh, um, nah, I'm still kind of full from lunch

But... you barely ate any lunch, though—

What? Yeah I did!

701

703

SNAP

So how are things with you and Nick?

Oh! Really good!

Haha... Sometimes I still can't believe he's actually my boyfriend

Really? Why?

I dunno... There was a time where I was super jealous of you because I thought you and Nick might... you know...

HA HA HA

There's no way that would have ever happened. Aside from the fact that I am absolutely not into guys—

—Nick's so in love with you it's a little unbearable to watch sometimes

Darcy was already out. We'd been dating for a while and most of our friends knew. But other people were starting to guess too.

At our school, "lesbian" was used as an insult all the time. I probably even used it once or twice when I was younger.

We were terrified.

It took me a long time to even feel comfortable calling myself a lesbian.

And for a while, we thought it'd be easier to pretend we were totally platonic.

I guess for a while it was easier.

But, in time, we got more comfortable being us.

We reached the point where we knew that whatever people said or thought about us, we knew who we were

And we loved ourselves anyway.

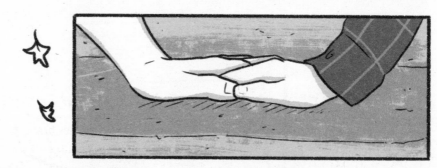

There they are!

Oh my God, d'you think anything happened?

I hope so, or Tao is gonna pine to death

It was fine.

So... did anything happen?

No!!? What was supposed to happen!? Nothing happened

Uh... okay

...

We just walked round the museum for a bit. It was nice.

719

But what about what she wants?

Sometimes it's worth taking a risk.

Why would she ever like someone like me, anyway.

She's so cool and interesting and beautiful. And I'm just me.

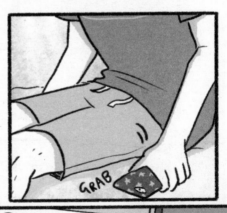

OPEN

?

What happened?

I tried to talk to him about Elle but I majorly fucked it up...

It's not your fault! He's really really stubborn.

722

725

726

729

730

731

Paris — Day 3

735

739

Weird.

I was thinking about it and... I don't think I even mind if people find out it was me.

Really?

Yeah.

I honestly think it'd be a relief to just... be out.

I was talking to Tara about it yesterday. She told me how she and Darcy came out and it made me feel like...

Even if things are harder when people know about us, we'll be okay, because we've got each other.

BOOP

SQUEEZE

That is literally the soppiest thing you've ever said.

Ha ha!! Oh God, it really is

746

RING
RING
RING
RING
RING

The person you are calling is unavailable. Please leave a message after—

...

Dating... who?

Each other. We're dating each other.

...

I thought... I thought you liked him but he's straight.

Yeah, same, but... it turns out he's bi and... now we're going out.

Oh! Well, that's amazing! What happened? Did he tell you this week?

...

Actually... it's been going on for a few months. We've been going out since April.

April!? Three months ago?

Do all our friends know?

Paris - Day 4

SIT

You okay?

I-I think I feel a bit ill today

Oh no! What's wrong? I have some paracetamol!

Or we could tell Mr Farouk?

I'll be fine. Just... not hungry.

763

767

BLINK

He's awake

heck

Hey

You're <u>sure</u> you feel okay, Charlie?

Yeah, I just- I haven't eaten enough today

CAFÉ MOLLIEN

And you didn't hit your head or hurt yourself?

No!! Nick kind of caught me

Okay. But if you feel ill at any time on the trip, you can come and tell me, okay? If you need to sit down or just want to rest on the coach, that's absolutely fine.

NOD

There you go, Mr Spring!

Get those in your belly!

...Thank you

We'll leave you to chill out for a bit, but— well, Nick can come and find us if you need us. Okay?

Thanks, sir

778

785

787

Run!!

Anyway, what did your dad want? I can't believe I didn't know he was French!

Oh yeah!! I wanted to try and meet up with him but he said he's too busy with work.

That can still happen eventually. It doesn't have to happen on this trip.

Yeah. You're right.

This has been stressing you out... You should have told me about it!

Yeah, I... I didn't want to make you worry.

I guess we've both been keeping some stuff to ourselves...

Haha! Yeah...

I love you

I love you

I love you

I love you

I love you

I love you

I love you

I love you

WHISPER

MOVE

I feel horrible about fucking up last year but I shouldn't pass that guilt on to you. I made a really stupid, idiotic mistake and you suffered really badly because of it.

I don't think I even understood how hard it must have been for you to come out to me.

So...

I will be a better friend and less of an idiot. I promise.

Okay ☺

Paris – Day 5

YAWN

...

That actually is a love bite, isn't it. Like everyone's been saying.

...

803

It's past eleven, boys. You should be in your room.

But sir, we were just—

Off you go.

You couldn't let them off? They're clearly dating.

They're dating?

...

815

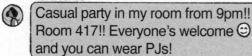

Tara Jones + 39 others

Tara Jones
Casual party in my room from 9pm!! Room 417!! Everyone's welcome 😊 and you can wear PJs!

Darcy Olsson
PLEASE BRING SNACKS IF YOU HAVE ANY. ESPECIALLY IF YOU HAVE PRINGLES

also I have vodka 🖐

Katie Lee
Yassss we'll be there!

Tom Jaeger
CAN'T WAIT

Aleena Bukhsh
omg darcy how did you get vodka

Darcy Olsson
i have my ways

Jared Lambe
YEEEEE LET'S GET LIT

Charlie Spring
we'll be there!!!!!!

That night...

819

Excuse me!! Those are my dimples!

Oh. Hi.

SHUT

821

825

BRUSH

whisper whisper

Ahem.

Sorry to interrupt your *very* obvious flirting, BUT-

832

Have you ever drunk alcohol before?

My mum lets me have a beer sometimes. Like at Christmas.

Lucky. My parents have never let me try it. They're so strict about stuff like that.

834

A little while later...

How do you get cold so easily!?

This is normal! I'm not a human heater like you!

Hey... what's going on?

SQUABBLE

SQUABBLE

838

839

I started to believe what they were saying

It made me really hate myself

...last year when everything at school was shit

TOUCH

849

850

Obviously dare.

JAMES

I dare you... to kiss James.

...

What!?!

I'm up for it!! Ha ha!!

You have to do it!! That's the dare!

Go ooon! It's just one little kiss!

855

SQUABBLE

SQUABBLE

SQUABBLE

I know who it was.

859

We're okay with being out.

We haven't been keeping it *that* secret anyway.

Ahem.

I hate to interrupt this very lovely moment, but—

865

SHUT

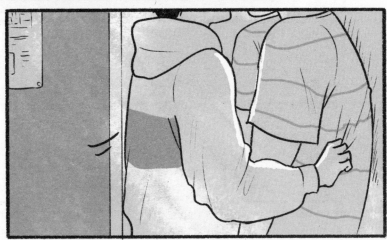

You came out to an entire room of people

Y-yeah, I guess I did.

868

I was scared about you having to deal with homophobic stuff.

PULL

And I guess I was scared about having that much attention on me ... again.

But now...

POOF

...

okay, maybe I'm still a BIT scared, but—

HIDE

871

Since the room is ours tonight...

874

881

887

889

890

SIP

Well... I suppose I should head down to reception and ask for some fresh sheets.

896

899

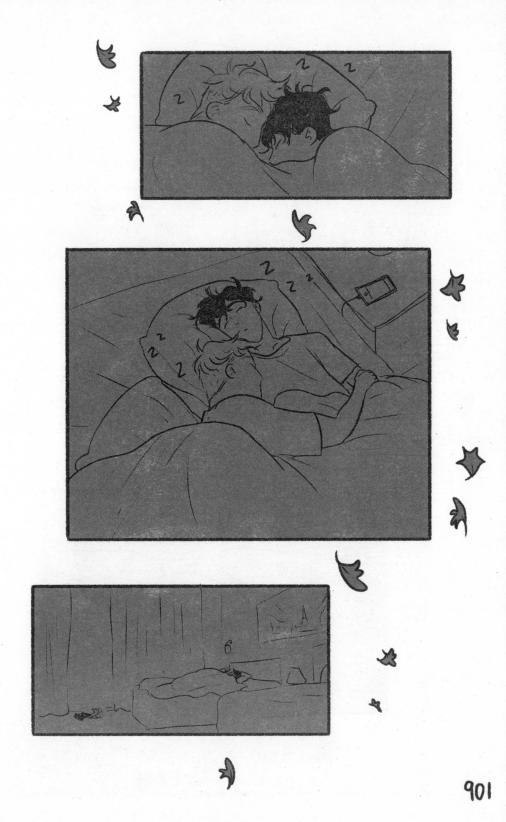

Paris - Day 7

Come on.
On to the bus.
We have a train to catch.

Um - Nick and Charlie -

Oh, hi Malik

Is it true you're dating??

905

909

Heartstopper will continue in
Volume 4!

Read more of the comic online:

heartstoppercomic.tumblr.com
tapas.io/series/heartstopper

Sunday 27th June

So tomorrow I'll be going away for a whole week to PARIS.
♡The city of love♡
Okay that's dumb. But I'm very excited!!!

None of my Year 11 friends are going, but I'll get to be with Charlie all day every day for a whole week, which is waaaaaaay better than being stuck at home now that my exams are over. And I really like Charlie's friends so I'd like to get to know them better.

I think I'm most looking forward to going up the Eiffel Tower. I always imagined it'd be super romantic to go up the Eiffel Tower with the person you ~~love~~ ~~like~~ love and take cheesy photos :)

very bad →
drawing of
the Eiffel Tower

27/6

I've just finished packing for the Paris trip tomorrow!! I've been excited about it for sooooooo long— a whole week to just explore and have fun with my friends. YAY!

Plus, me and Nick are sleeping in the same room!! I know we won't really be able to kiss and be couple-y much because other people will be around, but I'm sorta hoping we get to sleep next to each other and just chat about silly random stuff all night...

And I WILL tell Tao about us. I want him to know. Even though he'll probably throw a strop about me not telling him.

I CAN DO THIS.

NAME: CHARLES "CHARLIE" SPRING
WHO ARE YOU: NICK'S BOYFRIEND.
SCHOOL YEAR: YEAR 10 **AGE:** 15
BIRTHDAY: APRIL 27TH
MBTI: ISTP
FUN FACT: I LOVE TO READ!

NAME: Nicholas "Nick" Nelson
WHO ARE YOU: Charlie's boyfriend
SCHOOL YEAR: Year 11 **AGE:** 16
BIRTHDAY: September 4th
MBTI: ESFJ
FUN FACT: I'm great at baking cakes

NAME: Tao Xu
WHO ARE YOU: Charlie's friend
SCHOOL YEAR: Year 10 **AGE:** 15
BIRTHDAY: September 23rd
MBTI: ENFP
FUN FACT: I have a film review blog

NAME: Victoria "Tori" Spring
WHO ARE YOU: Charlie's sister
SCHOOL YEAR: Year 11 **AGE:** 16
BIRTHDAY: April 5th
MBTI: INFJ
FUN FACT: I HATE (ALMOST) EVERYONE

NAME: Elle Argent
WHO ARE YOU: Charlie's friend
SCHOOL YEAR: Year 11   **AGE:** 16
BIRTHDAY: May 4th
MBTI: ENTJ
FUN FACT: I like making clothes ♡

NAME: Tara Jones
WHO ARE YOU: Darcy's girlfriend
SCHOOL YEAR: Year 11   **AGE:** 16
BIRTHDAY: July 3rd
MBTI: INFP
FUN FACT: I love dance! (especially ballet)

NAME: Darcy Olsson
WHO ARE YOU: Tara's girlfriend
SCHOOL YEAR: Year 11   **AGE:** 16
BIRTHDAY: January 9th
MBTI: ESFP
FUN FACT: I once ate a whole jar of mustard for a dare

NAME: Aled Last
WHO ARE YOU: Charlie's friend
SCHOOL YEAR: Year 10   **AGE:** 14
BIRTHDAY: August 15th
MBTI: INFJ
FUN FACT: I want to make a podcast

NAME:
HARRY GREENE
WHO ARE YOU:
NICK'S CLASSMATE

NAME:
David Nelson
WHO ARE YOU:
Nick's brother

NAME:
Sahar Zahid
WHO ARE YOU:
Tara, Darcy, &
Elle's friend

NAME:
Mr Ajayi
WHO ARE YOU:
Art teacher

NAME:
Mr Farouk
WHO ARE YOU:
Science
teacher

NAME:
Nellie
WHO ARE YOU:
Nick's dog

Nick's room

view A

view B

Key features:

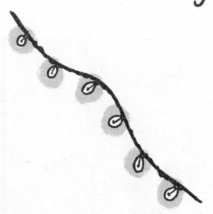

Fairy lights

Nick put up fairy lights in his bedroom one Christmas and forgot to take them down for three months. Eventually he decided he liked having them up all year round!

Bean bag

A comfy, cosy bean bag Nick's had for years. He sits in it sometimes but mostly it's Nellie Nelson's favourite nap spot.

Posters

Along with posters of his favourite movies, Nick has some posters of his two favourite sports: rugby and motor racing.

Charlie's room

View A

View B

Key features:

Electronic drum kit

Charlie started learning how to play the drums when he was nine. He doesn't have any particular aspirations to become a musician or be in a band, but he still really loves playing, especially to relieve stress!

Bookshelves

Charlie's favourite hobby is reading. He'll read any genre, especially if there are gay characters, but he finds Ancient Greek classical literature the most interesting.

Posters

Along with posters of his favourite bands, Charlie has posters of two of his favourite classic texts: The Iliad by Homer and Brideshead Revisited by Evelyn Waugh.

The First Day

a Heartstopper mini-comic

THE PREVIOUS SEPTEMBER...

I'm so nervous... What if I make no friends?

You will!

Just hang around the art department until you find some other girls who like painting and sewing and stuff.

That sounds pretty awkward, but... okay.

Well, you've still got us. You can text me any time!

It's gonna be weird. Us not eating lunch together.

Because you can't steal my Mini Cheddars any more?

Obviously. I'm gonna miss those Mini Cheddars!

The end.

THE HAIRCUT
A HEARTSTOPPER MINI-COMIC

one day in Nick & Charlie's future...

SNIP
How much did you just cut off!?!
You said you wanted it short at the sides!!
Yes but I don't want to be BALD.
You're not bald!!
I will be if you keep this up!!

Many minutes of squabbling later...

Look who finally gave in and let me cut his hair

 Omg that actually looks good

We did have one casualty though

 LMAOOOOO

 oh my GOD

 Nick's new career – dog stylist?

 I have confiscated the razor

The end

Author's note

Here we are in the third volume of Heartstopper! It feels like only yesterday that I had two thousand books stacked in my house, ready to be shipped to my Kickstarter supporters. We've come so far since then!

This volume starts with Nick and Charlie solidly a couple but with a lot to learn about each other. I strongly believe that the 'getting together' part of a romance is just the beginning and there's so much else to explore beyond that, and Nick and Charlie spent much of this volume getting to know each other on a deeper level, which has been such a joy to write. It was also wonderful to get to know some of Heartstopper's side characters in this chapter! Tao, Elle, Tara, Darcy, and even Aled all have a bigger role to play, and I hope we continue to get to know them better in the next volume.

This volume also touched on the more serious topic of mental health; in particular self-harm and eating disorders. Mental health and mental illness are topics that are very close to me and I explore them in all of my works, but here in Heartstopper I want the focus to always be on support, healing, and recovery. If you are struggling with any of the same issues, please do not hesitate to reach out to someone you love, just as Charlie has done, and/or a medical professional. You could also seek help and advice from an online support network, such as:

YoungMinds: https://youngminds.org.uk/
Beat Eating Disorders: https://www.beateatingdisorders.org.uk/
Switchboard LGBT+ Helpline: https://switchboard.lgbt/

Sending so much love and thanks to Heartstopper's online readers, my Patreon patrons, and the Kickstarter supporters! It's thanks to you that the series is able to continue.

To Rachel Wade, Alison Padley, Emily Thomas, Felicity Highet, and everyone else involved in Heartstopper at Hachette - thank you so much for making these books a reality! I'm so grateful to be working with such a passionate and dedicated team.

A huge thanks to my agent, Claire Wilson, who is my guiding light in the world of books!

And thank you, as always, to you, dear reader! I'll see you in the next one.

Alice
x

Collect the whole Heartstopper series!

Read more about Nick and Charlie...

Or read Alice's other prose fiction...

  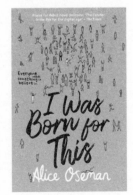

Please go to aliceoseman.com to find out more about the books and their content warnings.

Alice Oseman was born in 1994 in Kent, England, and is a full-time writer and illustrator. She can usually be found staring aimlessly at computer screens, questioning the meaninglessness of existence, or doing anything and everything to avoid getting an office job.

As well as writing and illustrating *Heartstopper*, Alice is the author of four YA novels: *Solitaire*, *Radio Silence*, *I Was Born for This* and *Loveless*, winner of the YA Book Prize.

To find out more about Alice's work, visit her online:

aliceoseman.com
twitter.com/AliceOseman
instagram.com/aliceoseman